DATE			

Eric the Red

Oxford University Press, 198 Madison Avenue, New York, NY 10016

Oxford New York
Athens Auckland Bangkok Bogotá Buenos Aires
Calcutta Cape Town Chennai Dar es Salaam Delhi
Florence Hong Kong Istanbul Karachi Kuala Lumpur
Madrid Melbourne Mexico City Mumbai
Nairobi Paris São Paulo Singapore
Taipei Tokyo Toronto Warsaw

and associated companies in
Berlin Ibadan

Oxford is a trademark of Oxford University Press

Text © Neil Grant 1997
Illustrations © Oxford University Press 1997
Published by Oxford University Press, NY, 1998
Originally published by Oxford University Press UK in 1997

Library of Congress Cataloging-in-Publication Data

Grant, Neil.
    Eric the Red: the Viking adventurer / Neil Grant; illustrated by
Victor Ambrus
        p.   cm.—(What's their story?)
    Includes index.
    1. Eric, the Red, fl. 985—Juvenile literature.   2. Northmen—
Greenland—Juvenile literature.   3. Geography, Medieval—Juvenile
literature.   [1. Eric, the Red, fl. 985.   2. Explorers.   3. Vikings.]
I. Ambrus, Victor G., ill.   II. Title.   III. Series.
G760.G7   1998
998.2—dc21
                                                                    97–42080
                                                                         CIP
                                                                          AC

1 3 5 7 9 10 8 6 4 2

ISBN 0-19-521431-5 (hardback)

Printed in Dubai by Oriental Press

Eric the Red

THE VIKING ADVENTURER

NEIL GRANT

Illustrated by Victor Ambrus

OXFORD UNIVERSITY PRESS

Eric the Red was born in Norway more than a thousand years ago. His father was a Viking chief, who owned land on a fjord, one of the deep inlets of the sea that make the coast of Norway so jagged.

There were no schools then, and Eric never learned to read or write. Instead, he learned the skills that all young Vikings needed. He learned to care for cattle and sheep. He learned how to build a barn, how to hunt and fish, and how to fight.

Above all, he learned the ways of ships and the sea. The Vikings were seagoing people, and every warrior had to know how to sail a ship and how to build one.

Viking chiefs were proud and warlike. They often quarreled, usually about land. When Eric was 15, his father killed some men in one of these quarrels. As a result, he was forced to leave Norway forever.

With his family and followers, Eric's father sailed to Iceland. Norwegians had first settled there a hundred years before, and already the best land was taken. Eric's family built their home at Drangar, a cold, rocky place in the far north that faced the Arctic Ocean. In autumn, icy winds piled up broken ice on the shore.

After a few years, Eric's father died. Eric was now a young man, tall and strong, with the red hair that gave him his nickname. He was a born leader, who was eager to own more land and command more men.

He also wanted a wife, and soon he found one. Her name was Thjodhild, and she was the daughter of a powerful chief who lived at Haukadal, in western Iceland. When Eric married Thjodhild, they left Drangar and went to live on a new farm in Haukadal. Their first son, Leif Ericsson, was born there soon afterward.

Quarrels among the Vikings were as common in Iceland as they were in Norway. Once, some of Eric's men started a landslide above a neighbor's farm, sending tons of rocks and soil crashing down on the farmhouse. Eric's men were caught and killed. The strongest law among the Vikings was the law of revenge, and Eric could not allow anyone to kill his men, whatever the reason. He attacked his neighbor, and the result was more killing.

Another feud began after Eric lent some wooden building props to a chief named Thorgest. Wood was valuable in Iceland, where few trees grow, and Thorgest refused to give the props back. Eric attacked his farm, and in the fight, two of Thorgest's sons were killed.

Things were getting out of hand. The council of chiefs met to discuss these killings, and voted to send Eric into exile for three years.

Like his father before him, Eric the Red was an outlaw.

As an outlaw, Eric could be lawfully killed. He had many enemies who would kill him if they found him, but he had friends, too. They kept him safe until he could escape.

He had to leave Iceland, but where would he go? Eric had already decided. He was planning a great adventure, a voyage of discovery. Eric believed that, away to the west, lay another country. Sailors who had been blown off course in that direction had seen mountains in the distance.

Eric had the same love of adventure that led earlier Vikings to travel thousands of miles in search of trade or treasure. He had their curiosity, too, the wish to find out more about the world. He dreamed of winning honor and fame, perhaps riches, too, by discovering an unknown country.

Secretly, he loaded a ship with food and supplies, and picked 30 of his best men as his crew. Late on a clear summer evening, his ship left the shores of Iceland, bound for the west.

They were sailing in cold and dangerous seas. Storms raised waves higher than the mast. Icebergs loomed out of the mist. Sometimes, a freezing fog blotted out the sun and stars, so they could not tell which way to steer.

N

GREENLAND

ICELAND

ERIKSFJORD

After several days they saw mountains on the horizon. Drawing nearer, Eric saw they could never land here. Masses of broken ice guarded the shore. He turned south. Soon they reached a rocky coast of deep inlets, just like the fjords of Norway. They camped for the winter near the mouth of what was later called Eriksfjord (Eric's fjord).

Remembering Norway, Eric expected to find good land at the head of the fjord. He was right. Between the fjord and the mountains lay miles of good grassland, with fresh water and even a few small trees. The sea was full of fish and the land full of animals whose meat was good to eat.

Eric had discovered the best land for a farm in the whole country. But he did not stop there. He spent three years exploring the coast. He found other places where colonists might live, some near Eriksfjord, some farther north. In his imagination, he could see the shores of Eriksfjord already covered with farms.

Eric had promised his friends in Iceland that, if he discovered a new land, he would come back and tell them. Now he decided it was time to keep that promise. He and his men repaired their battered ship and sailed back to Iceland.

In spite of all the dangers, Eric returned safely with every man who had set out with him three years before. He found that his old enemy, Thorgest, had not forgotten their quarrel. There was a fight, and Eric's men lost. But afterward, Thorgest and Eric agreed to end their feud. Eric had more important things to do.

Eric was now a famous man. News of his discovery spread from farm to farm. Many people wanted to learn more, and Eric was eager to tell them.

Like a good travel agent, he made the land sound as pleasant as he could. Although it was mostly covered with ice, he called it "Greenland" because, he said, people are more likely to go to a place if it has an attractive name.

People listened eagerly to his tales of easy hunting and fishing. A man could take all the land he needed, Eric told them, and never worry about fights with his neighbors.

The Icelanders were pioneers and adventurers, who had created one new country already. Now that Iceland was getting crowded, hundreds agreed to follow Eric to Greenland. It was a huge risk. They had to sell everything they owned and sail across unknown seas to a country where no human beings lived. But they trusted Eric.

In the spring of the year 985 the great Greenland expedition sailed. Twenty-five ships followed Eric out into the Atlantic. Each ship held about 40 people—men, women, and children. Their cargo took up a lot of room, because they had to take with them everything they needed, from knives and spoons to live cattle, horses, and sheep. They took food for themselves—dried meat and fish, cheese and butter—and bales of hay for the animals.

The ships were open to the weather, so everything had to be covered in leather to keep it dry. With horses snorting, sheep bleating, dogs barking, cows mooing, men shouting, and children crying, it was a noisy departure.

Only 14 ships reached Eriksfjord. Some turned back after losing touch with the rest of the fleet or because they lost courage when they sighted the ice on Greenland's east coast. Some sank in the cruel Atlantic.

ric had already claimed the best site, at Brattalid. His friends staked out claims on Eriksfjord, or on other fjords nearby. A few started a separate colony farther north. The richest men got the best land.

Although so much of Greenland was covered by ice, Eric had not lied. The land really was green. The animals grazed hungrily on fresh grass, while the women cooked over campfires, and the men began to build houses. They used stone and driftwood, covering the walls and roof with turf.

After news of Eric's settlement reached Iceland, more colonists arrived. The climate in Greenland was warmer than it is today, and farmers could grow some vegetables, such as cabbages. It was too cold to grow wheat or corn to make bread, but Icelanders ate mostly meat and fish. There was plenty of both. The reindeer and other animals had never seen humans before. They were not afraid of them and were easily killed.

The Greenlanders had no king, but there was no doubt who was their leader. Traders and other visitors called first at Brattalid. Eric entertained them in the Long Hall, where a hundred people could eat together.

One visitor was a young man named Bjarni Herjulfsson. Bjarni had set out from Iceland but got lost in a fog at sea. When the fog lifted, he saw land ahead of him.

He thought it could not be Greenland, because it had no mountains. He sailed north for a few days, then realized that he had sailed too far west in the fog. He had found another new country.

Eric was very angry with Bjarni, because he had not tried to explore the country. He talked to Leif and his other sons about it. One day, someone should visit this land of Bjarni's.

Leif had his father's love of adventure and his gift for leadership, but he was not so hot tempered. In about the year 999 he visited Norway. The king of Norway had become a Christian not long before, and he asked Leif to take the Christian religion to Greenland.

When Leif returned to Brattalid, he brought a Christian priest with him. After they had listened to the priest, most Greenlanders became Christians. The Christian god was less frightening than the old pagan gods of Norway.

Eric was growing too old for such great changes. He still believed in Odin, the grim and mysterious chief of the Viking gods; and in Thor, whose hammer caused the thunder; and in the terrible day of Ragnarok, when the world would be destroyed.

Eric's wife, Thjodhild, did become a Christian. That caused trouble, because Thjodhild refused to share a bedroom with a pagan and shut Eric out. Later, she had a church built at Brattalid.

To get away from these troubles,
Leif decided to make a voyage to the
land that Bjarni Herjulfsson had seen.

Leif was called "the Lucky," meaning lucky for
others, because he once saved many people from a
shipwreck. Other men were ready to follow him, but Leif
hoped his father would lead the expedition. Eric might be
an old man (he was about 50, old in those days), but he
was still the greatest man in Greenland.

At first Eric refused to go, but in the end Leif persuaded him.

On the day the ship was due to sail, Eric was riding down to the shore when his horse stumbled and he was thrown off, hurting his leg. To Eric this was an act of fate. In his religion, all things were ruled by fate, and fate had warned him that his voyaging days were over. Leif sailed without him.

Leif sailed in Bjarni's old ship with a crew of 35 men. They were gone for nearly a year. When they returned, Leif brought exciting news. They had found Bjarni's land and sailed south along the coast until they came to a beautiful country, with large woods and wonderful grass. His men had built houses and spent the winter there. It was so mild, there was hardly any frost. Cattle could spend the whole year outside. They also found wild vines, thick with grapes, and for that reason Leif named the country Vinland, or "Wineland."

The country that Leif had discovered was North America. The remains of some houses built by Leif and his followers were discovered in the 1960s in northern Newfoundland, Canada, at a place called L'Anse aux Meadows.

Eric listened to Leif's stories with great interest and perhaps some sadness, too. He knew he would never sail to Vinland. That winter, a sickness broke out among the Greenlanders. Many people died. Among them was Eric the Red.

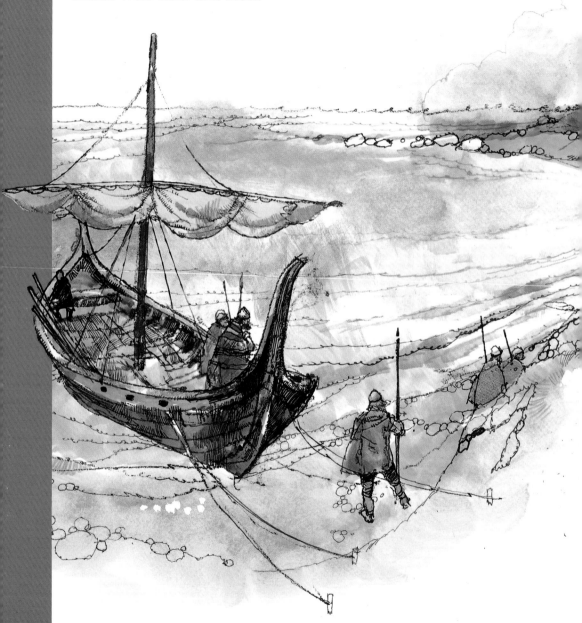

Many Viking chiefs were great warriors, and some were great explorers. Eric was both of these things, and more besides. He was the discoverer of a new land, and he was the founder of a new nation: Greenland. Long after he was dead the poets of Iceland wrote about his great deeds.

After Eric's death, Leif became chief. He often visited Vinland but never settled there. Christopher Columbus, who sailed from Spain to America in 1492, would have been astonished to learn that other Europeans had visited his New World nearly 500 years before him.

Eric the Red and the Viking sagas

The Vikings did not write books or keep records. During the long evenings, they told stories around the fire about famous heroes and warriors of the past. These stories were passed from one generation to the next until, many years later, the time came when they could be written down. It is mostly from these stories, which are called sagas, that we learn about Eric the Red and his family.

But the sagas are not history. We do not know how much is true and how much is made up. Most of what you have read in this book comes from two sagas, The Greenlanders' Saga and The Saga of Eric the Red. These were written in Iceland more than 200 years after Eric's time.

We do know a little about Eric and the Greenlanders from other sources. For example, in recent years archaeologists have discovered the remains of Eric's house at Brattalid.

Index